Places in the Mist

poems by

Laurel Chambers

Finishing Line Press
Georgetown, Kentucky

In life, a person will come and go from many homes. We may leave a house, a town, a room, but that does not mean those places leave us. Once entered, we never entirely depart the homes we make for ourselves in the world. They follow us, like shadows, until we come upon them again, waiting for us in the mist.

Ari Berk, Death Watch

Places in the Mist

*For Jerry, who has read every poem I have written,
and whose love and support have always lifted me higher.*

Copyright © 2022 by Laurel Chambers
ISBN 978-1-64662-867-4 First Edition
All rights reserved under International and Pan-American Copyright Conventions. No part of this book may be reproduced in any manner whatsoever without written permission from the publisher, except in the case of brief quotations embodied in critical articles and reviews.

ACKNOWLEDGMENTS

"Once in the City on Calhoun Street" previously published as "Once in the City" in *For a Better World 2016*
"Gypsy Night" previously published in *Within Us* (A Poetry Anthology in in Celebration of the Greater Cincinnati's Writers League 2020).
"Brown Girl Dead" previously published in *For a Better World 2021*

Special thanks to Karen Jaquish.
For the people at Women Writing for (a) Change, Cincinnati Greater Writers League, Pauletta Hansel, and the Cincinnati writing community, thank you for your inspiration and encouragement.

Publisher: Leah Huete de Maines
Editor: Christen Kincaid
Cover Art and Design: Elaine Olund
Author Photo: Mikki Schaffner

Order online: www.finishinglinepress.com
also available on amazon.com

Author inquiries and mail orders:
Finishing Line Press
PO Box 1626
Georgetown, Kentucky 40324
USA

Table of Contents

Cannon Avenue
Awakening on Cannon Avenue 1
The Golden Egg 2
Days of Hoboes and Campfires 3
The Wooden Box 4
The Knight at My Door 6
Night Noises 7

Lakewood Boulevard
First Time at the Dance 8
My Boat and Oar 9
Night Creatures Pushing Through 10
Sonnet of Shame 11
Morning at Columbia Beach 12
Ode to Patsy Ann 13

Calhoun Street
Once in the City on Calhoun Street 14
In My Boat Alone 15
Small Enough 16
Where Does A Woman's Anger Go? 17
Brown Girl Dead 18
For One Man 19
I am Being Unbuttoned 20

Seiler Drive
From My Kitchen Window 21
The Old Stone Church 22
The Lesson: For My Son 23
Betrayal 24
Gypsy Night 25
What Lies Beneath This Family Ground 26

Lincoln Road
Float Boat 27
September Walk on Lincoln Road 29
The Passing of the Plague 30
The Digging 31
Kindling 32
Dreams of Absolution 33
A Change of Vision 34

Cannon Avenue

Awakening on Cannon Avenue

On hot sticky nights
no breeze came off the lake
to rustle the trees or my bedroom curtains.
I slid to the foot of my little bed,
propped my pillow by the open window.
Sometimes, I awakened before the dawn.
The street below was dark and shiny
under the moonlight and fading stars.
Soon, the street lights turned off,
all at the same time,
like some wizard with one strong breath
blowing out every candle on the cake.
I watched the light crawl up Granger Hill,
the dark lawns slowly turning green.
Then the sun rose higher behind the houses
like butterscotch dripping over the roofs.
Most of my neighbors still in a deep sleep,
far away in a world of dreams.
All of the block quiet and at peace.
The silence was holy and mystical
like a quiet, empty church.
A divine grace would sink into my soul.
Soon, I could see the houses come alive.
McMann's kitchen light, soft and golden,
glowed like a lantern behind the trees.
Sanders' living room lamps blinked on.
The new day was waiting for us,
waiting for all of us to begin the noise of living.
I, with innocent eyes knew even then,
how wild and wonderful this world was.
How my life was beginning and would begin
again and again and again
at first light.

The Golden Egg

It is a lucky day
when I come home for lunch
and she is making Mrs. Grass's Chicken Noodle Soup.
She shoos my brothers to the back playroom.
Calls me to stand on the stool.
I stand next to her holding the wooden spoon.
Never more than in this moment
do I feel I am the favored child.
She opens the package and gives me
the magic egg, the flavor nugget
to hold gently, reverently in my hands.
I cradle it softly like a baby bird.
Knowing too early or too late a drop
from the nest means it will not melt
into a caramel colored cloud.
Together, we watch the water rise and bubble
like a tiny typhoon inside a silver pool.
The steam rises, she pulls me back.
My face too close. But how to pull away
from this wonder we create?

Then she begins her count, *Ten, nine,
eight, seven...* I am the astronaut
blasting from the earth, speeding to the moon.
I hear her call from the tower up above.
Are you ready? Now!
I gently drop the golden egg into
the boiling water. It spins and twirls
at a frantic pace swirling like blonde curls.
I stir it gently until the mystery occurs.
The egg grows small and smaller,
then it disappears.
The bubbling water now looks like honey.
I am such a wondrous girl
to make this magic occur.

The brothers come and she pours the soup.
They want the tiny skinny noodles.
I drink the broth like from a holy cup.
No crackers cracked or bread soaked in.
I have waited patiently for the golden egg,
the miracle my mother and I have made.

Days of Hoboes and Campfires

Escaping from our crowded city streets,
we children came in twos and threes
from Granger Road and Nelson Street.
Crawling under the broken fence in my back yard,
bursting like escapees freed into the green
of crazy old Lee Mason's field.
There, we took control, made up names
for all the places we did not own.
Sneaking where we were not supposed to go,
racing down railroad tracks by Sloane's Creek.

At our Apple Bend we once found
a dusty campfire, tree logs in a circle,
burnt black potatoes stuck on long sticks.
Hobos from the trains had camped there.
We put on broken hats and dirty scarves.
Stuck balls of store bread on our sticks.
Held them over the dead campfire.
Watched all summer for some hobo to slide
off the train and visit our shrine.

Terry McNamara with his mane of red hair
glowed like a fox above the tall grass.
His voice shouted at us to march in line.
Always the general in our wars,
like the war our fathers fought and won.
He led us into screaming battles
somewhere on the plains of France.

At Cherry Bend we had lookouts in the trees,
rusty canteens, a plastic cavalry horn.
Brought blankets and beads for the Cherokee,
rode bareback up the hill by their land.
In Mason's field we lived a hundred lives.
The days drifted away, outside of time.
We soared unleashed into that sky,
like bright kites without tails.

The Wooden Box

My father polished shoes.
Most Saturday nights before bedtime.
Carried up the little wooden box
with brushes, cloths, and a putty knife
from underneath the basement stairs.
Spread old Cleveland newspapers across
the yellow chrome kitchen table.
A surgeon with his tools.
Taking Timmy's crusted Buster Browns,
scraped out mud and grass around the sole.
He needs to wear his tennis shoes
when he plays down by the creek.
Another brother's not as bad.
Dipped his fingers into the polish can.
Spread brown oily paste from toe to heel.
Brushed back and forth, side to side,
top to bottom, until they looked almost new.
With my patent leather Christmas shoes
he had the magic of Vaseline.
Rubbed it in with a flannel cloth.
Buffed in circles with a gentle touch
until they shined like black glass.
For mommy he had the white polish in a bottle,
the wand with the little sponge on top.
The liquid looked like milky chalk.
Painted only the white parts of her spectator pumps.
Making sure to wipe away any polish
that leaked into the brown trim.
Took baby Tommy's white walking shoes.
They could be cleaned up too.
Brushed the wand across the scuffs and scrapes
until they faded away.
His turn was last with his business shoes.
Black paste swirled around,
he would spit into an old tee shirt,
rub around the toes over and over again.
It was the old spit shine
learned in the army and used for his boots.
The shoes would be done, lined up on the table

Daddy, Mommy, Scott, Laurel
Timmy and baby Tommy too.
Set to sleep the night away until they dried.
My father polished shoes.

The Knight at My Door

Your shy eyes would watch and follow me
at Edwards Park where we played after school.
Once, you asked to pull my sled up Sharkey's Hill.
Doubled decked them like an English bus.
Your sled on the bottom, mine on top.
Dropped ginger snaps on my table during lunch.
Your steps would slacken when I was behind,
waiting for me to catch up to you.
We would walk together down Tulley Street.

At Christmas time, my mother called.
Eddie Doyle is at the door for you.
There you stood like a frozen knight
who had galloped a hundred miles.
Pushed into my hands a tiny silver package,
a little pink bottle called Rose of France.

It took me years to learn
that words were often silent in the world of men.
Later, I would hear them speak to me
with flowers, sweets, rings,
and other sparkling things their love would bring.

Night Noises

Past the field behind my childhood home,
trains would travel through the night
like slow waves rolling on the track
with a constant rhythm of clickety clack.
Each train car would rumble past,
then the pulsing sound would fade away
into the dark and lonely night.

There was the loud grating, grinding sound
of giant trucks shifting gears
driving up the hill towards the Clifton Bridge.
That aching sound echoed three blocks down.
Mr. Mac's old Chevy chugged down the street.
He worked an extra shift, in need of sleep.
The car squeaked and rattled as he steered to the curb,
closed the car door lightly, not to disturb.
O'Donnell's dog Casey would yelp and woof
at some squirrel or bird outside their door.
Then Casey fell asleep and was heard no more.

Best of all was the music rising from my downstairs.
My mother and father talking at close of day
with all their work and cares put away.
Their voices floated up the stairs like a song,
kind, laughing, warm, and strong.
I could never quite make out their words.
It did not matter, it was the harmony I heard.

Lakewood Boulevard

First Time at the Dance

My eager body longed for the coming night.
Rinsed lemon juice in my hair to make it shine.
Sprinkled perfume in every secret place
only known to me.
Imagined how this dance would be
with bright lights flashing all around.
The drums and piano pounding loud.

Reds and blues bounced off the floor.
The air was salty, steamy.
My skin slick with heat.
I could feel my hips sliding
side to side underneath my skirt.
My eyes smiled at your eyes
that watched and promised me.
Every muscle moved in rhythm freed.
My body glowed with a feverish light.
I became a woman Phoenix,
taking up a fiery flight.
Rising from the ashes of a girl.

My Boat and Oar

The sea is cool tonight
cuddling around my feet.
Summer waves sway into the land
in a soft and steady beat.
The beach wraps me in its golden sand
and holds me to my home.
Should I get my boat and oar
or should I stay on the shore?

The water is blackberry blue
far out in the distant sea.
High in the midnight sky
stars like pearls peek through.
The bottom there is deep and wide
with mysteries unknown.
Should I get my boat and oar
or should I stay on the shore?

Through all the centuries
of unsteady human time,
people have stood at the edge of sea
on confused and tangled nights.
They have prayed to gods in the sky
to send a clear and certain sign.
Should they stay on the land so dry
or row out to the deep and dive?

Night Creatures Pushing Through

I turn on the lights in every room
but all is dark and all stays still.
I cannot find a candle or a match
to light the way in this woeful black.

But the night creatures, they push through.
From every corner I can feel them move.
In the air, I can hear them breathe
but in the dark they cannot be seen.

Nasty ghastly goblins of the night
with stiff boots, knives aimed high.
They march and plunge into my mind,
doubt, despair, sorrow, fright.

They parade with flags upon my soul,
join forces, make nests, take control.

Sonnet of Shame

I have known the sad fallen face of shame.
I have seen the harsh verdict in their eyes.
I have felt the pain climb like crimson flames.

I have smeared a sweet smile to hide my cries.
I have said quick words, longed to take them back.
I have watched how fast a crushed flower dies.

I have run and tripped across the slick tracks
where all my secrets spilled across the ground.
Tumbling from my glass jar now full of cracks.

Blazing rage has surged in me without sound.
I have shrunk from your words that rang with blame.
Flailed in your laughter till I almost drowned.

I could not stand strong and say my name.
I have known the sad fallen face of shame.

Morning at Columbia Beach

Sometimes the sun is like a sleepy eye
rising slowly in the morning sky.
Taking time to absorb the beauty after night.
The vastness of the sky with unseen planets
somewhere out there spinning wild.
Sparkling stars hidden in the bright daylight.
The earth sculpted into rocky peaks.
Rivers like blue ribbons swirling around
the dense, great, grassy greens.
Oceans thundering with high waves
then collapsing into peaceful pools.
Creatures of yellow, red, and blue,
jump, fly, crawl, coo.
Beasts of brown, spotted, white, black,
run, leap. Roam the earth in packs.
The tropical wind from the South blows in
whispering a soulful tune.
All of this, all of this.
All of this is here for you.

Ode to Patsy Ann

Oh, how you blasted into a room
like a midnight ride with the top down
speeding across the Lake Road Bridge.
You walked so wide down our tight streets
wrapped in your proud ripe roundness.
Some spicy beat in your step as you moved,
never knowing there were any rules.
All the promises that dripped from your words
we tried to catch in our young excited hands.
You believed it was all a gift
not to save or to embrace
but to scatter across the stream like spring leaves.
Your velvet cape to Nora for the dance.
Your jar of shells to Martha to make her vase.
Your red scarf to Nancy to wear with her brown coat.
Your warm skin and wet kisses to all the boys
just because they wanted them.
How I secretly cheered for you with my timid heart
standing in silence in the back of the room.

Calhoun Street

Once in the City on Calhoun Street

I lived in the bowels of the city, once,
long ago when I was young.
I'd open my window to feel a breeze.
All I heard was the siren's scream.
The dirty wheezing of the city bus,
heaved and choked, the breaks squealed.
Like a monster coming down the street,
it roared and clambered, destroyed the peace.
I closed the window, it killed the breeze.

I lived in the bowels of the city, once,
long ago when I was young.
On a cold hushed winter night,
snowflakes large as flowers
cascaded like a waterfall for hours.
Underneath my window seat,
a light was shining on the street
where an old black man, rocked and moaned
holding onto the lamppost, covered in snow.
He's drunk, they said, *maybe full of junk.*
A fool to be out and about, not home.
His sadness echoed through my rooms.
What harm could such an old man do?
I rushed outside on that dark icy night.
He was blind and had dropped his cane.
Freezing, frightened, all alone,
his white cane buried in the snow.

I lived in the bowels of the city, once,
long ago when I was young.
And on a cold and snowy night
I walked an old man home.

In My Boat Alone

I have been out in my boat alone,
many miles away from home,
when the night slammed down from the sky
like a door leaving the stars behind.

The moon filtered through a tiny crack.
My sails collapsed, my heart went flat.
I lost all hope of rowing back.
None of my lamps could hold the light.
I begged the moon to swell more bright.
I trembled in the darkness of that night.
For I was out in my boat alone,
many miles away from home.

The winds came up rough and high
crashing into my boat, side to side.
There was a loud, thundering sound
as the wind knocked my boat around.
The sky dumped water all that night.
Dreams of land vanished from my sight.
For I was out in my boat alone,
many miles away from home.

Then morning brought a gentle rain.
A yellow sun lit the sky again.
My boat started floating up and down,
to a soothing rhythm it had found.
Although my broken body ached,
I was able to hold the oars and take
a steady pace, steer my boat around,
to a fleck of land my eyes had found.

When I finally pushed my boat ashore,
I was a different person than I was before.

Small Enough

If I could shrink down to the size of a butterfly,
fold my wings from corner to corner
like a freshly laundered sheet.
Become so tiny you could tuck me in
a slender crack on your skin.
Tell me, dearest.
Would that do?

If I could be like all those desperate girls,
who live on water and carrots for years
weighing every single grain of rice.
Their only desire to become so thin
in hopes that they will disappear.
Tell me, dearest.
Would that do?

If I could be a grain of sand on the ocean floor,
ten thousand feet of water on top of me.
With big ships riding on the waves,
sailors knowing which way to go
but never seeing me below.
Tell me, dearest.
Would that do?
Would I be small enough
for you?

Where Does a Woman's Anger Go?

When you go to your room
keep it.
Keep it in the back of your jewelry box
behind the tarnished silver bracelet
and the broken string of pearls from France.
Lock the jewelry box with the little copper key
with the green tassel and purple ribbon.
Hide the key in the stocking drawer.
Fold it with a scarf beneath the black tights.

When you go into the world
hide it.
Hide it deep inside your blue coat pocket
underneath the old wrinkled handkerchief,
mixed up with the murky oily pennies,
stray buttons, and broken pencil stubs.
Hide it in the bottom
where it becomes stale and hard
like long forgotten cookie crumbs.
If the drycleaner finds it, flipping pockets inside out,
he'll just throw it away with the worthless junk.

When you stand at the stove
cook it.
Cook it slowly till it simmers like a thick sauce.
Scrape it from the bottom with the wooden spoon.
Then turn the switch to high.
Let it bubble and rumble into a boiling rage
where the steam races up the walls and floods the air.
Flip it and fry it until it sizzles, cracks, and pops
and everyone knows not to come near.

When you start to speak
swallow it.
Swallow it though it's jagged like a peach stone
that scrapes as you swallow it down.
Gulp it fiercely until it's pushed inside your chest
where it lodges and throbs each time you breathe.
Then a burning acid creeps into your mouth
that makes you cough and wheeze.
Then push it down, down to the dark silent deep.

Brown Girl Dead
Inspired by the title of a poem written by Countee Cullen

It happens every few years.
An American princess is on the news.
Long straight locks of blonde or brown.
Pixie nose, creamy skin.
Smiling with straight suburban teeth.
She's gone missing.
Was last seen jogging on a street,
walking on a beach, leaving the store.
Was supposed to be somewhere
at a certain time. Never came.
Never called. Not like her at all.
The hurt, the worry settle deep,
making it hard for us to breathe.
A daughter, a sister, a girlfriend we see.
We pray, light candles, form search parties.
Paste her picture in a thousand places.
Reach out our hands to the grieving parents.
The mother and father who never sleep,
pleading to the cameras every night.
Just bring her back, just bring her back.
The police work every single clue,
hoping to bring justice do.
But after days and months, sometimes years.
The truth comes in.
It is exactly what we feared.
There are vigils and holy words
that we offer for our dead girl.
But when a brown girl
was supposed to be somewhere
at a certain time. Never came.
Never called. Not like her at all.
Her story is never on the news.
Her picture never posted for us to view.
Maybe her family gets a word or two,
not on TV every night pleading for her life.
We're never asked what we can do.
After days and months, sometimes years.
Her truth comes in.
But it is news we do not hear.
Someone, somewhere found a brown girl dead.

For One Man

I once swam beyond Huntington's Reef,
plunged into the ocean deep.
You walked up and down the beach
watching my hair weave into the waves.
Holding a fisherman's rope, calling my name.

Once, I dropped my heart into your hands.
You wrapped it in fleece not silver bands.
Rubbed me with lavender oil to sooth the pain.
Honored all my gossamer dreams.
Pushed the door open so my soul could breathe.

I do not know what will come for you and me.
Will we spin together into eternity?
I do not know if the moon will always hold its light.
Will the stars always shine at night?
But I will always know how much one man loved me.

I am Being Unbuttoned

The golden autumn sun
flows through the curtains
on this lingering afternoon.
A caramel glow on everything.
The tiny mother of pearl buttons slide easily
with a gentle push from your fingers.
Your tongue swirls around my neck
seeking the salt and the sweet.
Your hands move slowly down
slipping across my awakened skin.
Then with the letting go of each button
a new space welcomes you.
There, a pink flower blooms and spreads
across my breasts warmed by your breath.
A hot flush covers me.
Your hands move slowly down,
another new space unwraps for you.
Here, your lips are like feathers brushing
stroking some secret spot.
There is exciting music vibrating in my heart,
Celtic drums and dancing flutes.
My flesh melting into liquid.
Some primordial chord throbs in me.
My breath heavy, thick, and rising.
All of my body turns to you.

Seiler Drive

From My Kitchen Window

The sky is brushed a watercolor blue,
a vast flannel blanket floating above the land.
Crisp, starched clouds like sails
glide slowly across a calm lagoon.

One brown Thrasher warbles from a high branch
whistling in eager anticipation.
Joyfully calling out to her lover,
I am back. I am back.

Silver knobs shine on the fingers of trees.
Threads of yellow- green sprout
from the brown sodden ground.
The whole earth stretches and groans
in the birthing of a new Spring.

Wherever you are my children,
all of the world is bursting
with hope for you.

The Old Stone Church

You have loved me with wide patient arms
like the open doors of the old stone church.
You have beckoned me into the stillness
where white candles glow in the daylight time.
The sunlight streams through stained glass widows
like your spirit filtering into red, yellow, and blue.
You have whispered blessed words that sound like prayers.
Here, the wooden floor still vibrates with sacred hymns.
The air has an ancient holy smell and when I take it in
every breath, a sweet release, my troubled soul at peace.
You have loved me with wide, patient arms
like the open doors of the old stone church,
where I have known and honored you.

The Lesson: For My Son

The evening rain fell softly all the night before,
a summer shower in the warm air.
That morning, my little son went out into the yard
to the world where he was the one in charge.
He gathered up all his building tools,
plastic knives, cups, bowls,
broken wheels from wagons,
twigs, branches, dented spoons.
Then kneeling in the soft mud,
he carved a river into the earth
where floating leaves turned into boats.
He piled up dirt like mountaintops
covered them in rocks.
He packed the soil in broken flower pots
flipped them upside down
with one on top of the other.
Then a skyscraper soared from the ground.
Twigs braided together became a bridge.
There were houses made of stone.
By the early evening, my son had built his town

That night, a hard rain pounded down
with cold air and loud, rowdy winds.
In the morning, my little boy rushed out
to save his little town.
With chubby fingers, cups, and bowls,
he tried to take the water out
to save the buildings that had melted down.
But the soil sifted through the flowerpots
like liquid earth, it wouldn't hold.
With frantic hands and old tin cans
he made a damn to hold the ocean back
but it collapsed like sand.
I did not want to be the one
to walk out to the yard that day.
Did not want to be the one
the one that had to say.
Sometimes, what we love gets broken
and it cannot be fixed.

Betrayal

That sad scene comes every spring.
The small Oklahoma town where
the fierce tornado touches down.
A broken bicycle hanging from a tree.
The ground looking like a tangled sea
of shattered branches, shards of glass.
Fragments and pieces of all things
that once were whole and complete.

One house with an entire wall blown away.
A private bedroom, cracked, exposed,
like a young woman whose skirt
is caught by a strong wind as she walks.
Her leg revealed for all to see.
An innocent doll with a missing arm
drowning in a dirty puddle of rain.
Cars and trucks flipped like coins.
The landscape of these people's lives
once so neat and secure, destroyed.

Like the people of the Oklahoma town,
who once trusted in the summer sky.
Our hearts were wrapped in trust with you.
Then your lies crashed down on us,
capsizing the order of our lives.
With those people we stand confused,
full of doubt in this world unrecognized.
Like them, we remember picnics,
crayon colored kites flying in the sky.

Like them, we search through the wreckage
longing for some truth we cannot grasp.
Desperate for something to embrace.
An old photograph still intact.
A pot unscathed that still can cook.
A young boy's missing cowboy boot.
The neck from a violin without a scratch.
But none of these can bring faith back.

Gypsy Night

I am leaving you in your own pool of tears,
where you float around
in the soft, warm, consoling waters
of your sweet sadness.

I heard music last night echoing over the mountain.
A rough fiddle gone wild.
A hard clicking of heels on a wooden floor,
beating like a feverish drum.

I am wearing a dress of bright peacock feathers.
Crushing cherries to rub on my lips.
I will learn to swing my arms high and low,
to rise with the wind.

Hurry, jump up!
I will be going tonight.
Leave your cloak of sorrow behind.
The stars that light the path are sharp and bright.
We have so little time.

What Lies Beneath This Family Ground

There are landmines buried here
deep in this family ground,
under patches of green grass,
beneath clusters of blue Phlox.
Hidden during hot wars and cold wars,
before long and short battles.
Concealed in times of silent struggle.
Some clashes so long ago, they are forgotten now.

Still, no one dares run across this land
on the first day of Spring
with excited, reckless steps.
Slipping and sliding across the dew.
Too many stories echo in this earth.
Too many visions erupt, too much to stir up.
A flying limb, a shower of bloody dirt,
A trusting heart blasted
into a hundred pieces
flying up into the smoky sky.

Maybe, some mine sweeper will come
with army gear, steel toe boots and helmet.
Point with a mine plow to breach a path
while swallowing every whisper.
Perhaps, we could follow him in single file
taking fragile baby steps.
One after another, after another, after another.

Lincoln Road

Float Boat
    "The child is the father of the man." William Wordsworth

Young boys were playing in the pool today.
Someone placed a giant float in the water
at the deep end by the bay.
Those boys came dashing, splashing to that place,
possessed by the vision to turn that float into a boat.

Some jumped on and tried to paddle to make it go.
But the float spun round and round
bumping into the side of the pool,
trapped in a corner, unable to move.
Till one boy, too small to paddle, took his place,
sat upright on the back, began to kick his feet,
and became the motor on the stern.
That float turned into boat began to churn.

The other boys then took their cues.
Moved to the sides of the float, sat upright too.
Their bodies knew what they had to do.
Used their arms like oars, hands cupped the water
then pushed it through.
That float turned into boat began to move,
slow and swirling it rumbled through.

The oldest boy crawled to the front,
anchored himself facing the bow,
knowing someone had to take control.
Then he shouted in perfect time, *more, more, more,*
like the coxswain with megaphone
chanting out loud, clanging like chimes.
Then those oarsmen pointed their fingers, started to dig
deep into the water, moving the float ahead.
Their arms still smooth, soft like baby skin
but showing curves where the muscles begin.

With motor roaring, coxswain shouting,
they shoveled that water with such might
that float turned into boat, began to glide,
fast and smooth across the water
like a magic carpet ride.

I could see the passion pounding in their eyes.
They were pirates on the sea stealing treasures.
Sailors on the ocean weaving through the wreckage.
Fishermen being pulled by whales.
With all that they were seeing, they pushed every speck of being.
That float turned into boat sped so fast it seemed to fly.

Oh, beautiful boys, who will sail many boats in your time.
Rides will be smooth, tough, rough, unkind.
Remember how today with vision burning in your eyes,
Moving together in perfect time
You launched your boat into the sky.

September Walk on Lincoln Road

The autumn sun slides through the cracks,
sifting through the early morning black.
It blooms like a candle over Meyer's Hill
melting like butter over browning trees,
telling us to breathe before winter comes to be.

Inhale the crisp chill riding on the air.
The earth turning, change is everywhere.
The bright light of the summer sun
fades every day. Brown moves into green.
Embrace this time in the world of In Between.

We are weary from the weeks of lusty greed.
Stuffing our souls with everything we need,
blossoms, birdsong, flowering fields.
The icy silence waits up ahead,
where souls murmur, no words are said.

Let us go and walk under this rusty sky.
where birds sing farewell before they fly.
Rosy leaves still drift down from trees.
The moon is a golden plum in the purple night.
We need not bury nuts or pull the quilt up tight.

This is the time before the losing of the light.
Days become shorter, nights grow long.
There still is time to find where we belong.

The Passing of the Plague

How will it be when we first crawl
out from our dark, lonely caves?
The long fearful winter of Covid passed.
Our bodies soft, sagging in places
gone slack from the tight constraints
of our gloomy cocoons.
Our souls empty, ferocious appetites
hungering for the human touch.
Hoping to catch a whiff of breath
from someone standing close.

How will it be when we are naked again,
our faces finally unmasked?
Will we watch in amazement as rouged lips
dance to form words?
Mouths wide open, heads slung back.
Some laughing girl across the table leans
into his shoulder. Warm bodies rub
against each other with no laws of restraint.
Will it be like "before" when it all comes back?
How will we measure what we have lost?

The Digging

Strange and worrying sights
made me leave my bad last night.
Looking to ease my troubled mind,
I pulled out the rusty lantern
from underneath the attic stairs.
Took my fur hat from the closet hook.
Covered my hands in thick wool gloves.
Pushed my feet into my old tight boots.

Across the frozen snowy land
I began to trudge, lantern in my hand.
A tiny shovel tucked inside my boot.
Then, I found a small patch of earth
underneath a tree, still green,
where I could dig and kneel.
I took the shovel with anxious hands,
pierced through the crusty seal.

I began to dig and dig and dig
through layers of cold hard earth.
The star clock ticking through the night
The moon dripping down its silver light.
I kept digging and digging in perfect time.
For I believed that if I dug deep this time,
there was a holy place that I would find
where the beautiful bones of hope did lie.

Kindling

You and I rise early.
The harsh wind creeps through the glass
of the window in this chilly winter room.
I dice dried cherries and peaches to steep
in the simmering water for morning tea.
Steam rises with a fruity smell of summer
flavoring the December air.
You poke and prod with sooty tools.
Slide the large log on the bottom,
scatter around dry twigs.
A flash, the shadow of the fire splashes on the wall.
You like to start the day with a wild blaze,
then give it time to settle down.
We sit and sip our tea together
crowded in the brown velvet chair,
our toes tingling near the fire.
We both look out the icy window
watching the frost slide down
the branches of our locust tree.
The sun rises with a glittery light,
the snow now glazed and sparkling.
If only I had known years ago,
this is enough.

Dreams of Absolution

You float from your celestial realm
down to this earthly world,
uninvited, unwelcome, unwanted.
You stand in my bedroom, a spirit girl.
Amber ringlets, a faded brown dress,
like a child in an antique tin photograph
transformed from a pallid old woman
with a sour mouth, a venal heart.
Fearful, you stand at the foot of my bed
grasping the post with slender fingers
watching me as I sleep.

In the midnight hours you come back
with a child's wide eyes that implore me
with an aching sorrow.
A look I do not remember seeing, even once,
in your thin grey eyes while on earth.
The gaze you spread upon me is thick,
packed tightly with layers of remorse.
The weight of it almost smothering.

Sometimes you peer around my bedroom door
afraid to enter the room.
I do not let you in.
I am no saint.
But I am exhausted from your disruptions.
The sword I carry is meant for you,
but in the darkness it pierces me.
I finally forgive you. I forgive you.
Not from some soft patch in my heart.
Not because of some ancient moral law
carved into stone, written in a holy book.
I forgive you so this will end, and
you will not come back.

A Change of Vision

There are cataracts forming on my eyes.
The lens, heavy with protein does not open
wide like when it was a window full of sky.
Once, there streamed all the shafts of sun.
The lens now a rusty gate, dull, hinged tight.
Jeweled colors fade and old stars are barely lit.

They say the light will change to hazy grey.
The street lamps already tall cloudy candles
glowing like amber sticks with halos of mist,
like gaslights on old streets where lovers kissed.
The night sky is wooly black with a tired face
sighing above on the pale yellow moon.

Let the young ones have the dazzling light
with their smooth skin and thick hair
that moves and dances with the wind.
Everyone gets to be young one time.
Let them strut everything bright, alive.
Explode like fireworks on a summer night.

See them jump, speed down the street.
Their eyes see lines and boundaries.
I walk slowly now, the path is blurred.
I see strange things in this dimming world
of shadow where mystical shapes emerge.
I do not miss the time when all I saw was clear.

Laurel Chambers has called Cincinnati her home since graduation from college. Her poetry has been published in *Within Us* and *For a Better World*. She was awarded second place in The Greater Cincinnati Writer's League Poetry Contest 2017. *Places in the Mist* is her first chapbook. She believes that in our hurried and booming world, poetry can help us slow down so that we can hear the words rising from each other's hearts. Laurel holds a Master's Degree in English from Xavier University and has taught English at the University of Cincinnati and Xavier University along with McAuley High School and other area high schools. She is active in the Cincinnati writing community and has served on the board of Women Writing for (a) Change.

www.ingramcontent.com/pod-product-compliance
Lightning Source LLC
LaVergne TN
LVHW041603070426
835507LV00011B/1273